AF254536

Chell Navarro

Sister of the Heath

LILY POETRY REVIEW BOOKS

Copyright © 2020 by Chell Navarro

Published by Lily Poetry Review Books
223 Winter Street
Whitman, MA 02382

https://lilypoetryreview.blog/

ISBN: 978-1-7347869-0-3

All rights reserved. Published in the United States by Lily Poetry Review Books.
Library of Congress Control Number: 9781734786903

Design: Martha McCollough
Cover Art: Jeanine Cobler

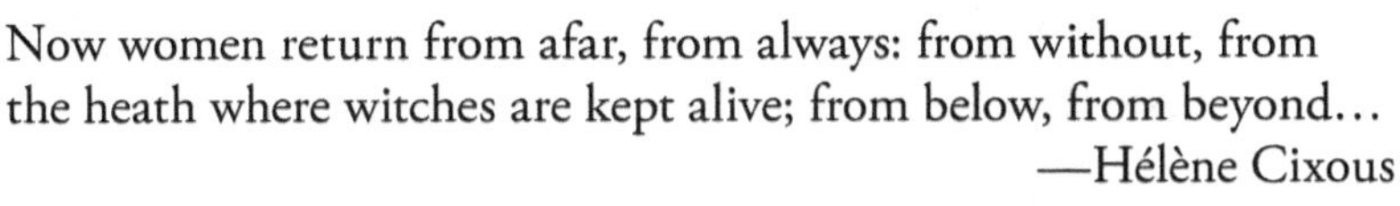

Now women return from afar, from always: from without, from
the heath where witches are kept alive; from below, from beyond…
—Hélène Cixous

wake up

she said

it's time

to reclaim

the lost

witch within

witch as name

for wise and

kind witch

for knowing

power

as energy.

the lightning

on edge

of the heath

is our magic,

our portent

Table of Contents

—*drawing No. 40, 1934. Georgia O'Keeffe*

From the Sea
—*with lines borrowed from The Laugh of the Medusa by Hélène Cixous*

fathoms deep
chasms briny
& female folds

into sinew folds
into cleft
folds only She can

speak to the dark
as aspect as in occult
as in sea of phantasms

what's the difference
between ocean & sea—
depth I say or boundaries

a world all our birthing
manifest no longer
manifest these waves

these outbursts I am
not a victim I am
a Medusa fresh out

of the sea I am
not a monster I am
not a fiend I am

a single-grooved mother
I have tongued an ocean
rife with unheard songs

Spring's Furies
—for Cynthia

Naked, sun-struck on slim limbs
you flaunt pink lipped blooms.

Tepaled to your center nectary, musk
floats in the shiver of early spring.

Tough carpels protect your covetous
cargo, redolent in twists of ascent.

Older than bees, the first of flowering
trees, beetles ravage your anthers savage

with intent. The night will cool your fevered
corruption. The morning will open you

wide, expose the tender
bud, displayed before summertide.

Poem about a Myth

She isolated herself
in a hall

of mirrors, spread out
all her tools,

explored with an artist's eye
the hidden

shadows and crevices
of the body—

garden with a bee's view
of the flower.

—*Abstraction IX, 1916, Georgia O'Keeffe*

About Her Kiss

This morning
before daylight
we hike Columbine Trail

The dew and sweet sap
cling to her hair. Later,

lying there—
one arm thrown back
face half turned—

her red mouth
kisses the shadows.

It all looks warm with sleep.

ECHO

Sound reflects
your acoustic light.

I want to hear
your name skip off

the canyon walls.
I want you to say yes.

I'm sorry.
I want you [still] alive.

We floated the Rio
Grande Gorge that last year

amazed at the corn-flower sky,
and watched crows soar.

So fluid our laughter
resounding off the granite

cliffs. Now I watch
the flow from the bridge above

and drift. The spring melt roars
out like your life. Rapid as the river.

Far from Home
—for Zaelia Lou

She picks the conch shell
from a pile in the terra cotta pot.

Thousands of miles from its home.
The shell spills sand

from its center. She wants to crawl
in, cup a beach in her hands.

Listen to the prose of the ocean—

Tell me about your emptiness.
Tell me about the moonrise.

How blue is your home?

Solitude Tastes Like Opium
—Adam Zagajewski

cloved in waiting

a forbidden blue

rose to cup a bite of poppies

tears into iron sleep

awakes such velvet ardor

midnight: a den with no moon

my Assyrian dream

floats on trails of smoke

so lucid quite what flying must be

fluent myrrh tars exquisite

flowering Asia

lulls me towards alone

I arrive home & taste some

spoonful of another self

& laud the bitter bouquet

Nexus of a Mythomaniac
—from Autoportrait by Edouard Levé

Solitude keeps me consistent. Is that lie really true?
Go see if I'm over there.

I feel like an impostor whose obscene
novelty disgusts me. My amorous states

bring two types of betrayal, simultaneous
lies. I would like to have myself hypnotized.

When I look out a window I feel no nostalgia
for childhood or Bach or a spring snow storm.

I cannot perceive the delay in mirrors
or the last time it was yesterday.

The last time it was yesterday,
I could not perceive a delay in mirrors

or my childhood, or Bach, or a spring snow storm.
And when I close the window, I feel no nostalgia.

No reason to lie. I like myself hypnotized.
Betrayal brings two types of betrayal.

Simultaneous novelty disgusts me.
My amorous states, like an imposter,

obscene. Go see if I'm over there. Solitude
is persistent. Constantly my lies ring true.

Effigy in Water and Glass

a sparrow strikes again and again against
its own reflection

you can't love someone
unless you completely annihilate yourself—

the pane never seems to crack
the bruises though

                                        ~ ~ ~

    deep tissue wounds don't heal, by nature
    the sparrow learns to survive, risks

    a fated leap from the nest
    death by a waiting predator or flight

                                        ~ ~ ~

I stare too long into the stream
a beloved portal—

I want to peer into you
                a reflection of our interior world—

heed the wings fluttering under a watery skin

          the stream casts a cool second glance
      grinning face of the Worm Moon

         the surface of it winnows
     with a desire for flight, a desire for destruction—

                                        ~ ~ ~

The current moves on;
         the moon teases
              the face peppered

with the wraith of wheeling sparrows

Mutable Day Dream

A pasture of clover buzzes from beneath;
dragonflies swarm as she pauses in the heat.

She looks straight up into the sun, blinded
by the sting of high noon. It's summertime

and horses mow the meadow one bite at a time,
their tails slaughtering flies—

the sound snaps to their hides like a willow switch—
They issue tremolo breaths between the whips.

Here are subtitles for a mutable daydream:
The poet suffers random bouts of grief.

Horses. Do they have a strong sense of self?
What would they do if their love spell failed?

Is there a link— a lyrical track to alone?
What if we never find a way home?

Brief Respite from the Rain

She believes she is herself, which isn't complete madness, it's belief…
a surface of water in an uninhabited world…
you wouldn't think of her form by thinking about water…
                              Mei-Mei Berssenbrugge

sidewalk puddles ponding
after the rain

reflect trunk & limbs
a slight dawn of sky

peeks of pinks & blue
nimbus springs

the scent of warm wood
steeps the air

my antithesis falls
into a better universe straddled

between seasons the spectre of
a looking glass I gaze in

& remember I am
water in a younger world

Chickweed
—for Mom

mouse-eared taproot sprawling
delicate, the white bloom

short-lived in spring

what the violet patch don't claim
the chickweed does

look at the countryside field
booming with color—

whites & purples & blues
this season shouldn't be a war.

constant gardener,
you fight the insidious threats.

you destroy the predators
but sometimes the invaders win.

when I was a kid
we'd sit in a mass of clover

chewing on chickweed buds,
like small goats searching

for the illusive four-leaf clover.
someday we won't have the farm.

the history of all of us
will be buried under a shopping mall—

or god forbid
a church. all the animals

& grebes, the creatures we tamed—
the creatures who tamed us—

you must embrace the ugly too—
it won't eat you.

look, some of us survived.

—Drawing No. 9, 1915, Georgia O'Keeffe

Poem with a Headache

Monsoon's comin'—

Ahead of it haboob consumes the valley.

Sepian blindness—

In every crack sand punishes to a fine finish.

And then the rain washes through the arroyos.

Blinded
—after Anna Akhmatova
for Amy

We empty another bottle to get
fucked up and bleary.
We know no other way
but looking into the bottom of a glass—

warped selves—twin images
fight for what's left of sight.

Our cigarette smoke blinds us
in a veil of usual ghosts. I see
what might have been. You see
a future choice. Behind a door

double chained. Deadbolt locked.
You hear that? Thief. Lover.

It comes to steal what's left
of what we can abide. The heart
is dead although the muscle keeps
beat. Even in the waning hours

the drink in us sings:
I love I love I love

Poem about a Late Obsession
—to Juan Hamilton

find a new medium to work

idle hands
form new ways to see

the flywheel throwing
New Mexican red

clay in my hands smooth his hands
smooth cool glide

quickening his breath
warm at the nape of my neck

his arms around
me guiding my desire

a vessel of rough work
spinning near the end

remain. stay. relevant.

wic̆e-tung

the secret to invisibility
you don't find

until you pass
fifty-five

it's a superpower
gifted to

the Crone from
the Great Mother

witch means wise
in the oldest

tongue means the oldest
language

of the First Men
and *woman*

woman because we
are infinitesimal

in a world
of men that holler

I can tell you things I've done
in my unseen state but

*How do you spell
tongue in the mouth?*

The Dance
— *after what if daddy were home*

cloaked-thrust dance loops lack
light heat of breath

a swain's shadow embraced past an instant
then there go back

against the beam blocked by the swoon
slow tango it was

death I danced on over death then dipped
the gleamed toe of

my stiletto in
the gap and tapped tapped

tapped at the grim air mid-stream
slipray of blithesome crypt exposed

where the shadow careens
transient shroud

in my eye slowed its stride
turned light-blinded back

my neck dank of death
dance stopped swung slack

--Blue lines, 1916, Georgia O'Keeffe

One Blue Line

It looks like rain.
I can smell it coming

far beyond Wheeler Peak
out on the high desert

plane. A lightning rod
cracks open

the monochromatic night.

I can no longer
get along without blue.

Incandescent

rattled death, the absence
of a pulse.

this is how you left—
moth dusting the porchlight.

the absence—how the last breath
fills a space outside
.

the body. Blinks and dims.
The soul escapes with a *tink*

of the Tungsten filament—
the dust of moth-wings cling.

Willow
  —for Maria

Each leaf, a corpse of summer.
As they fall, so fell you.

The willow tree's slender branches
shed simple leaves. Feather veined,

serrated and blue—All I saw of you
from the precipice of the grave.

Silver edges. No flaws.

Ekepepotamena [escape]

Having been breathed out / you will go
your own way / among dim shapes.
--Sappho

Gloaming,

in the corner of my eye.

The frozen

moted light. Early winter

flexes

its muscle in the doorway

of your body

or something more liminal.

The snow—

a wrested *escape of a soul*

into

nothingness. You, a drift

of a million

flakes. Fall into a sparrow's

nest. Yes

you were right there.

ECHO

outside myself

a ghostly comfort

I pour your ashes over the side of the boat
a gust of wind brings you back

the dust clings to me

I yell your name
into the river gulch

MARIA

my voice returns
hollow

three times

Ma-   'ria---ia---a---}}}

only the fog

floats over water

an acoustic shift sounds like

nothing

Sister of the Heath

I met you
when you were closed-up

petal-furled
tiny magenta mouth

and with the warmth
of a spring day

before a thunderstorm
you opened up

exposed your
lavender light eye

to the humid world
ready for the picking

ACKNOWLEDGMENTS

"Poem from the Sea" Fragments borrowed from *The Laugh of the Medusa* by Hélène Cixous.
"ECHO" first published in *Sprung Formal XII*, 2017.
"Far from Home" first published with http://typishlycom/2018/04/16.
"Nexus of a Mythomaniac" Found poem created from the text of *Autoportrait* by Edouard Levé
"Brief Respite from the Rain" first published at *Nature in the Now* Blog, a publication of *Tiny Seed Press*, and published in *Tiny Seed Literary Journal*.
"The Dance" An ekphrastic poem based on the collage *What if Daddy Were Home* by Glyneisha Johnson. Box Gallery Ekphrastic Exhibit May 2018.
"Ekepepotamena [escape]" from Anne Carson *If Not, Winter: Fragments of Sappho*
All references to Georgia O'Keeffe drawings and some phrases: *Some Memories of Drawings* by Georgia O'Keeffe, published by University of New Mexico Press.

C.D. Wright was the inspiration and I borrowed her use of "Poem…" for the titles of some of the O'Keeffe series of poems.

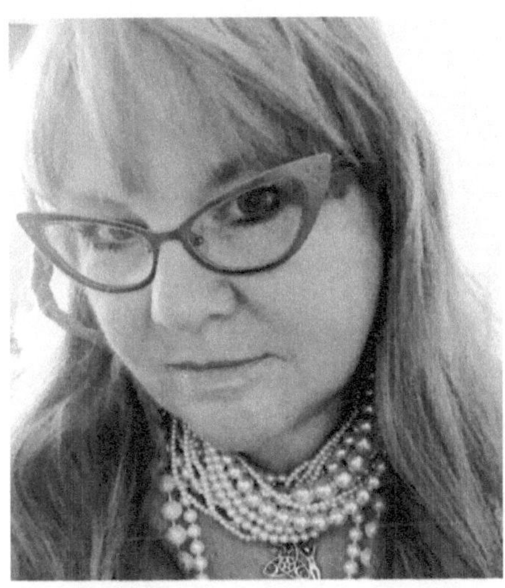

ABOUT THE AUTHOR

Chell Navarro is a poet, zine maker, and waitress. She holds an MFA in Creative Writing and Media Arts from the University of Missouri-Kansas City. Navarro founded Savage Torpor Poetry and Press in 2018. She resides in Kansas City, MO with her beloved familiars—dogs Patchouli and Alice, and Sappho the cat.

COVER ARTIST

Jeanine Cobler studied, enjoyed, and collected the work of other artists for many years, and began to create her own in 2002. She has a BA from the University of Missouri at Kansas City, and has studied at the Kansas City Art Institute and elsewhere. To see more of her work, visit www.jeaninecobler.com

www.ingramcontent.com/pod-product-compliance
Lightning Source LLC
Chambersburg PA
CBHW032135050726
47590CB00008B/3099